Oceans of Thoughts

Book One

An Inspirational Walk through the Inner Self,

Life and History

To: John
PR From the HEART
Thank you for
your interest in the
Oceans of thought
Peace
Rosleo McClean
3/16/2022

Rosalind Severin McClean

Oceans of Thoughts

Book Cover Design: Pawan Kumar

Logo illustration by Rene Y. Sumagang

Publisher: Rosalind Severin McClean

Printed in the United States of America

ISBN: 978-0-578-78220-1

Dedication

This book is dedicated to the memory of my sister Yvonne, who during her time here on this sphere truly encouraged me to keep writing. She admired my writing style and had confidence that my work as an author was meant to be. Yvonne, I listened to you then, and I must express again sincere gratitude for those years of encouragement.

TABLE OF CONTENTS

Acknowledgments 1

Unforeseen Directions 3

Introduction 6

Yvonne 8

Floods Of Emotions Series...15

Dominica...53

Passionate...69

Some Of My Convent School Memories In Roseau, Dominica (Da), ..84

Inspirational 126

About The Author 157

Acknowledgments

I have been writing towards this goal for many years, and now I feel very appreciative to be the author of this book. I would like to thank some people among others for their time and support along the path: my daughter Malti McClean for her computer skills and expertise; Jennifer Fadelle Johnson, Jennifer Rawle Davis, Constance R. Shillingford, my mother Mrs. Audrey Severin, my sisters Carol Abraham and Alice Dupigny, and my nieces Dr. Giselle S. Volney and Sharlene Wyke for their support; and Dennard Mitchell for his mentorship and his confidence in my ability to be an author.

I appreciate all of you.

Rosalind Severin McClean

OCEANS OF THOUGHTS

Unforeseen Directions

Blessings all! Jah bless in unimaginable ways which surface through unforeseen directions. To all my many readers on this Oceans of Thoughts project, I thank you and appreciate your keen interest in my work, and I absorb all the positive currents that would pulsate from your thoughts. Jah bless, and power from the good director of inspiration, that uses the creative mind energy of Oceans of Thoughts in His own way and on His own time to channel this work.

I was very carefully instructed one afternoon by a philosopher, Anthony Jones, who spoke some awakening words to me that surprised my being. He looked at me and said, "I see you channeling that Higher energy from the Higher source into your writing. I see you focusing. Thank you for inspiring me with that good inspiration. You inspire many people." Those words struck a chord as it arose from an unforeseen surface created by Jah hand, who continues to speak this kind of energy to His people through the creative waves of Oceans of Thoughts.

In the mighty name of Jehovah Shammah, the Lord who is present who sits on Oceans of Thoughts, I thank You for Your mighty direction on my work. "My thoughts are not your thoughts, neither are your ways My ways" (Isaiah 55:8). I will praise You with my whole being of Oceans of Thoughts. I will tell of all Your marvelous works. The words of the Lord are pure words, like silver tried in a furnace of earth, purified seven times.

OM to the greatest I AM. The Alpha and the Omega. The God of plenty on Oceans of Thoughts. The Omnipotent One.

Peace. Namaste!

Rosalind Severin McClean, October 9, 2019

Introduction

Book One of the *Oceans of Thoughts* series is finally complete. Remarkably, this book has been long overdue.

Oceans of Thoughts is beautifully written. It is crafted around some of my life experiences and, according to many reviews, the variety in my work can relate to everyone from young adults to seniors, to students to professionals of all careers.

In this book, the well of messages that pulsates through my work in poetry captivates the minds and hearts of the readers. *Oceans of Thoughts* is also referred to as a work of inspiration and a source of history.

I encourage everyone to read this book and to join me on the wonderful journey of *Oceans of Thoughts*.

I thank you all for supporting my work.

YVONNE

Preface

For my sweet sister Yvonne as we celebrate the anniversary of her third year in Eternal Bliss: April 6, 2020.

You came again, dear sister, on your sunny anniversary, fluttering busily and pecking at my window.

I knew it was you, as no other distinctly pecks at my window at 8 a.m. every year, on April 6, since you transitioned.

I heard your coo, but this time I just waited to see you. Peck, peck, then you flew, blowing miracles in your flight.

Rosalind Severin McClean, April 6, 2020

"In the inmost of our soul there is the world of the
Spirit and the world of the Spirit is free.
Where the Spirit of the Lord is, there is liberty."

MAJJHIMA NIKAYA

IT'S YVONNE! SHE CAME

SWEET COOING!

You gently sat, on the iron rail
Delightfully coo, coo, cooing
Right across from my window
You cooed and waited
And cooed and waited
You cooed for quite a while

We followed your sweet cooing
And looked for you
Through the large sunny windows
That bright and beautiful morning
We hustled from window to window
My daughter and I
To get a glimpse of you

And there you were
Sitting and patiently waiting
And coo, coo, cooing heartily
Across, on the iron rail
Staring, directly through my window
Until you saw that I saw you

Oh yes!
It's Yvonne, she came
You knew that I would have called you
Whilst on this earthly sphere
So, in the midst
With angelic purpose
You visited at my window

Mysteriously
Beautiful little dove
With Divine ability
You gracefully cooed
Pearly, piercing bright eyes
To let me know that
You are still there

Then you fluttered
And you flew away
To the transparent
Blue heavens path
On this gorgeous
Crispy sunny morning
Of May 21st, 2019
At 8 o'clock
All signs of amazing wonders
All signs of favorable presence
All signs of heart fulfilling blessings
All signs of Divine bliss
All signs of Divine consciousness
All signs of Divine wisdom
All signs of the great OM!
Oh yes!
It's Yvonne, she came
Peace!

Rosalind Severin McClean, May 23, 2019

OCEANS OF THOUGHTS

FLOODS OF EMOTIONS SERIES

Part 1

A Tribute to Mrs. Yvonne Severin Volney

Preface

Blessings all! I am indeed very thankful to everyone who is supporting me on this wonderful journey. I have written a three-part series of poems inspired by the grace around my sister Yvonne. I read a couple poems from this series at an Open Mic event in 2017, which received wonderful reviews. The next poem in this series I wrote as a birthday gift to myself on May 23rd, 2019. I thank God for His guidance on this journey of writing. Peace!

Rosalind Severin McClean, May 23, 2019

"Beyond the senses is the mind, and beyond mind is reason, its essence.
Beyond reason is the spirit in man, and beyond this is the spirit
of the universe, the evolver of all.
And beyond is Purusha, all-pervading, beyond definitions.
When a mortal knows him, he attains liberation and reaches
immortality."

KATHA UPANISHAD

YES! SHE'S MY SISTER TOO

Floods of emotions
Ocean waves flow
Rivers of waters
Tears overflow

What happened!
Alarming fit
Strange sacrifice
Daring conflict
You headed the team
Knowledge and wit
Tight-lipped
Momentous tip
Yes! She's my sister too.

Continuous conversations
We shared
Intelligent
Creative beam
You stuck by my hip
With sister glue
We were unseparable
We were very close
Everything it seemed

What happened!
You halted
On pressured feat
Yes! She's my sister too.

A gifted pianist you were
From childhood throughout life
You gave of yourself
You gave to family
Pure selfless service
All through your life

You were brilliant
In your prestigious career
Diligent through your work
And in music and dance and culture

You were a rare gem
With a sweet gentle love
And humble spirit

You were specially chosen
With a genuine heart
And strong faith

Yet!
You suffered through
The stigma of
Unfavorable plights
Shadowed with
Your beautiful personality
Your spreads of joy
Your precious smiles
Your hearty welcomes

You told me all
You told me all
Yes! She's my sister too

Last text message from you
"Going to the hospital
Don't call me nuh"!
Words unforeseen
No previous warning
Of your failing health
Distress unmeasured
Discontentment prevailed

Say hi and bye
Hurtful cry
She must not be stressed
Shocked! I complied
Yes! She's my sister too

Numerous phone calls
Unanswered
Numerous text messages
Unreturned
Numerous inquiries
Unfulfilled
Moments of continuous plea
Undelivered
Travel plans
Unresolved
Conflicted demands
Overall

Tell her, tell her
She can hear, she can hear
Tell her, tell her
It is me, it is me
Precious moments, irreplaceable
Yes! She's my sister too.

Then she was told
She stared
Looking
At the sound of my name

At last! She knew I was calling
At last! That fateful morning
At last! She heard my name
At last! Just one more time
At last! Peace
In transition
Yes! She's my sister too

Floods of emotions
Ocean waves flow
Rivers of waters
Tears overflow

Rosalind Severin McClean, June 24, 2017

FLOODS OF EMOTIONS SERIES

Part 2

"A spirit is within, which by deliberate skill you must separate from the body."

THE GLORY OF THE WORLD, Robert Valens Rugl

OH! ANGEL DOVE

Floods of emotions
Ocean waves flow
Rivers of waters
Tears overflow
Oh! Angel Dove

Astound in color
Stripes black and white
Moving gently
Beautiful in flight
Gliding right over my head
Landed!
Stunning!
One step in front of me
Not once, but twice
Two mornings blossom
Oh! Angel Dove

Eyes of shiny pearl
Reverent delight
Rear jewel sight
Pure Precious Dove
Honest emotions
Knowledge untold
Truth in motion
Wisdom Behold
Oh! Angel Dove

You came again
Oh! Beloved Dove
At my window
With streams of three pecks
Mother's Day, early morning
Surprise! What's that!
Came peck, peck, pecking
In pure delight

Quiet, eased to peek
Oh! Mystic Dove
You saw that I saw you
Eyes of pearl
Then you flew
Oh! Angel Dove

Floods of emotions
Ocean waves flow
Rivers of waters
Tears overflow

Rosalind Severin McClean, May 24, 2017

FLOODS OF EMOTIONS SERIES

Part 3a

"Just as dreams are unreal in comparison with the things seen in waking life, even so the things seen in waking life in this world are unreal in comparison with the thought-world, which alone is truly real."

HERMES

DREAMS REVEAL THE STORY Part 3a

(May 6-16, 2017)

Floods of emotions
Ocean waves flow
Rivers of waters
Tears overflow

Emotions turn into dreams
Dreams reveal the story
The story of what's not seen
Not seen with the naked eye
We see in dreams
With the spiritual eyes
We look for messages
From those mystical dreams
For answers to emotions
Of sister, Yvonne dear

The sixth day of May
Very early that morning
Scene of that dream
Set in the family home
All windows and doors
Mysteriously wide open
All around the house

I awoke in the dream to find
A tremendous flow of wind
Blowing across the land
The sun had not awakened
In the glowing dawning sky

My father was present
In the dream
But did not utter a word
I dashed across the corridor
To alert my sleeping mother
To close the French windows
Which were wide opened
All around the house

I saw a long slender swing
Made with white rope
That hung outside
The front bedroom windows
Of the neighbor's pink house
A brown-skinned little girl
A beautiful child she was
Clearly three years old
Accompanied on that swing
By a graceful adult woman
With a light-skinned complexion

They were both
Chuckling and laughing
And swinging merrily
While facing our family house
Then suddenly
The child stood up on the lady
While they were still swinging
And began to step up
Climbing on top of her

We look for messages
From those mystical dreams
For answers to emotions
Of sister, Yvonne dear

Rosalind Severin McClean, May 4, 2019

FLOODS OF EMOTIONS SERIES

Part 3b

"Purge me with hyssop and I shall be clean:
wash me, and I shall be whiter than snow.
Make me to hear joy and gladness;
that the bones which thou hast broken may rejoice."

PSALMS 51:7-8

DREAMS REVEAL THE STORY PART 3b

(MAY 6-16, 2017)

Floods of emotions
Upon another quiet night
Another astonishing journey
A dream to journey through

I saw this cosmic sunny day
That birthed
A startling loud noise
That stunned the air
I looked outside in dream

There was a white pickup van
Out of control it seemed
It crashed through
The white fence
At the front of our home
And launched itself across
The flowered front lawn

There was an assortment
Of white coral stones
And white coral gravel
In white crocus bags
Carefully heaped
At the back of that van
There was no one in the van
But two tall men
Stood on the hill
Right outside our home

We look for messages
From those mystical dreams
For answers to emotions
Of sister, Yvonne dear

Rosalind Severin McClean, May 4, 2019

OCEANS OF THOUGHTS

FLOODS OF EMOTIONS SERIES

Part 3c

"All the rivers run into the sea, but the sea is not full;
Unto the place from whence the rivers come, thither
they return again."

ECCLESIASTES 1:7

DREAMS REVEAL THE STORY PART 3c

(MAY 6-16, 2017)

Floods of emotions
Upon another faithful night
Another astonishing journey
A dream to journey through

A brown-skinned young girl
Driving a Bedford truck
In clear daylight
Trees in the wooden trunk
Of that truck
The truck turned right
At a sharp corner
And disappeared down a road
I ran down the stairs
To look for her
The brown-skinned young girl

There was no sign of her
But an unpaved road
Lined with dry grass
On either side
The vast blue Caribbean Sea
Seen in the distance

I went back up the stairway
Where a crowd gathered
At the front of
A quaint wooden house
One person held
A small silvery
Sparkling green ornament
And attempted
To gift it to me

A young man greeted me
And walked me through
A small lit piano room
Of another building
I exited that building
Looking for her
But I never saw
The young girl again

We look for messages
From those mystical dreams
For answers to emotions
Of sister, Yvonne dear

Rosalind Severin McClean, May 4, 2019

OCEANS OF THOUGHTS

FLOODS OF EMOTIONS SERIES

Part 3d

"Beyond the senses are their objects, and beyond the objects is the mind. Beyond the mind is pure reason, and beyond reason is the Spirit in man.
Beyond the Spirit in man is the Spirit of the universe, and beyond is Purusha, the Spirit Supreme. Nothing is beyond Purusha: He is the End of the path."

KATHA UPANISHAD

DREAMS REVEAL THE STORY PART 3d

(MAY 6-16, 2017)

Floods of emotions
Upon another revealing night
Another astonishing journey
A dream to journey through

I saw an enormous
Shining white air bus
The words "Con Clair"
Written on the left side of it
Written large in a celestial blue
A blue never seen before
With the naked eye

"Con Clair" flew straight
Towards the family home
Gliding smoothly down
From far over the hill
It was stunningly breathtaking

The large shining white air bus
Slowly dipped down on approach
Over the front side lawn
Of our house
"Con Clair" written clearly
On the left side of the air bus
"Con Clair" flew low over
The beautiful side lawn
Windows sealed shut

I was standing on
The long spacious verandah
In full panorama of the vessel
Looking at this shining
White air bus in awe
"Con Clair" glided low
Slowing down towards
The back end of the verandah
While it passed me

It glided upwards
Over the valley
That stretches from beyond
The extended garden
Of our family house

It glided in the direction
Of the magnificent
Green tropical mountains
Which were seen
In the far distance.

I watched the name "Con Clair"
Until it disappeared
She sat inside that air bus
I knew then
She was gone

We look for messages
From those mystical dreams
For answers to emotions
Of sister, Yvonne dear

Floods of emotions
Ocean waves flow
Rivers of waters
Tears overflow
Peace!

Rosalind Severin McClean, May 4, 2019

OCEANS OF THOUGHTS

DOMINICA

Preface

After witnessing the amazing Thanksgiving Concert live from Dominica on September 19, 2019, staged in commemoration of the second anniversary of the massive hurricane Maria which totally devastated the island, I feel honored to have been inspired in November 2013 to write this heartwarming poem about our beautiful nature-island, the Commonwealth of Dominica (DA).

Rosalind Severn McClean, September 19, 2019

"When thoughts arise, then do all things arise.
When thoughts vanish, then do all things vanish."

HUANG PO

A BEAUTIFUL TESTIMONY ABOUT

DOMINICA (DA)

A West Indian woman
Saw me today
Not by chance but
By Divine appointment
Last name seemed familiar
Yet unknown
Eyes soft but far
Deep in thought she was
So pleasant
So kind and simple
So humble and graced

She asked
"Where are you from?"
"Dominica," said I
Smiling in response
"And where are you from?"
I asked, then
The beautiful testimony began

She said
"I am from Antigua
But I want to retire in Dominica
Dominica is so luscious and green
I want to build my house
And make my home
And garden in Dominica
I have traveled all over the world
Africa, Europe, London, Hawaii, Alaska
The West Indies
All over America
(And the list went on)
But I have never come across
Another place like Dominica
Dominica is a beautiful place"

She went on
"I have been to Dominica
Many, many times"
And she named
Wesley, St. Joseph, Goodwill
Jeffers Lane, La Plaine and
All over Dominica
"That is where I am going
I just love the island
I will send all my retirement funds
To Dominica
And just live there"

She said much more
Words like music
Like sweet vocals
Words so clear
So honest
So faithful
So pleasant
So true

Listening ears
Curiously interested
Stopped to glance
Astonished they were
As the scene unfolded
Yes! Her beautiful testimony
Wrapped in waves
All powerful and lyrical
Like celestial chimes

So happy I was
To meet her
Name not familiar
Yet Divine
Dear to heart
With an angelic voice
With a genuine spirit
With a sincere smile

She blessed my presence
With her gracious aura
And her inspiring
And beautiful testimony
And her delightful experience
About our wonderful island
Sweet Dominica (DA)

OM! Peace!

Rosalind Severin McClean, November 20, 2013

OCEANS OF THOUGHTS

Preface

This poem has a slight touch of the Dominica (DA) dialect, using 'de' for 'the' and 'dem' for 'them.'

It was written during the aftermath of Hurricane Erika in 2015, which severely ripped through the island causing massive destruction.

The rapid emotions and aroused anxiety felt during that period embedded the Rock that inspired this poem.

The Rock is Higher than I. Jehovah Jireh, the Lord, the provider.

Rosalind Severin McClean, August 28, 2020

"The sacrifices of God are a broken spirit:
a broken and contrite heart —
these, O God, You will not despise."

PSALMS 51:17

SHOW DEM, SHOW DEM! DOMINICA (DA)

Glorious starry skies

Beguiled atmosphere

Crowded field activities

Immense

Intense

Intriguing

Courageously

Goddess smiles

Free of that space

Brush of prepense

Wealth and waste

Hurried

Hopeful chase

Enticing

Embarked

Two o' clock

That quiet morning

Lord!

No more

Not at all

True audacity face

True perfect pace

Goddess chose

To leave

Sing! Courage

Sing! Freedom

Sing! Message

Sing! Praise

Her Master's

Choice and call

Oh! Dominica

Created by [1]Jah hand

A tip of that wealth

For de small island

Expose de love

Extend dem hands

Expand dem hearts

Conscience fused

Wake dem up

---

[1] JAH: God

Transparent protective being
Transcendent spiritual realm
That favored Goddess
On favored call
No more revel
No! No more
Not this time
Not at all

Papa Bon Dieu[2]!
Dominica Island in crisis
Hurricane Erika savage
Powerful!

Complete catastrophic destruction
De whole Dominica Island
Total!

Complete hurricane devastation
De whole Dominica Island
Mayhem!

---

[2] PAPA BON DIEU: Father God

Complete wretched chaos
De whole Dominica Island
Unbelievable
Unfathomable
Unimaginable
De Erika wicked!

Show dem, show dem
Show dem, show dem
Unravel their conscience
Dem in de abundant world
Unveil their eyes

Show dem, show dem
Show dem, show dem
Unknot their hands
Untie their hearts

Show dem, show dem
Show dem, show dem
Share de abundance
Spread de wealth

Oh Lord!
Apprise that crowd
To acknowledge the cry
Inspire the multitude
To answer the call

Shine Divine light
Upon the cause
Bless Dominica Island

Shine Divine light
Upon sacred call
Deliver Dominica Island

Shine Divine light
Upon the nation
Rescue Dominica Island

Yes Lord!
Shine Divine light
Upon the land
Save our beautiful
Breathtaking
Dominica Island

Show dem, show dem

Peace!

Rosalind Severin McClean, September 3, 2015

OCEANS OF THOUGHTS

PASSIONATE

Preface

This poem is written with a certain level of depth and completeness. The context and experiences relate to many households around the world.

From the many reviews received I believe that my work on this poem has reflected through several persons. One must be mindful of their actions and always extend some gratitude for the extension of creation in their lives.

As Sadhguru once said, "Self-transformation is not just about changing yourself. It means shifting yourself to a completely new dimension of experience and perception."

Rosalind Severin McClean, August 29, 2020

"Desires are only the lack of something, and those who have the greatest desires are in worse condition than those who have none or very slight ones."

PLATO

UNDER THE UMBRELLA

Under the umbrella of sisters
But we were never friends
Preferences and prejudices
Created childhood complains
Created childhood pains
Created childhood stains
Created childhood strains
Still!
Stretching for decades
We were never friends
Under the umbrella of sisters

Continuously comparative
Mistakenly competitive
For everything!
Cluttered motives
Developed spiteful jealousies
Unforeseen anger
Unsuspected character
Hidden behavior old
Stretching for decades
We were never friends
Under the umbrella of sisters

Anxiety and frustrations
Pure bitterness and corruption
Spitting vinegar every motion
Scarcely honey in conversations
Abrupt and discourteous
Constant hasty-tempered blocks
No communication!
Vexing disfavored intentions
Daughter's mean frustrations
Oh Lord!
We were never friends
Under the umbrella of sisters

Conveniently short memories
And shamefully rude
Mother and daughter both
Call of nature's wrath
Plight on desperate path
Oh gosh!
Like teacup on saucer
Carrying their backs
Tight and secured
How quickly they forget
Oh Lord! Oh no!
We were never friends
Under the umbrella of sisters

Sister! Relationship craved for
Sister! Embrace dreamed for
Sister! Access courtesy longed for
Sister! Lasting compassion yearned for
Skillful ears could hear
Sister's voice is REAL
Educated and intelligent
Favored, born first
Courageous
Psychological twist

Hear me, Lord!
Heal our hearts
Heal our thoughts
Heal our wounds
Healing Hands
Give us peace
Give us love
Give us unity
Great OM!
Strengthen this sisterhood
For we were never friends
Under the umbrella of sisters

Rosalind Severin McClean, October 31, 2018

OCEANS OF THOUGHTS

Preface

From the intensity of family prejudices and traditions to the thoughts of family pretenses and trust.

I was encouraged to craft this poem as a voice of the hidden influences in the nest of families.

II Timothy 1:7 says, "For God has not given us a spirit of fear but of wisdom and sound mind."

Rosalind Severin McClean, September 1, 2020

"Do not be deceived, God is not mocked; for whatever
a man sows, that he will also reap.
And let us not grow weary while doing good, for in due season
we shall reap if we do not lose heart."

GALATIANS 6:7, 9

PRETENSE TOGETHERNESS FAMILY DYSFUNCTIONAL

Pretense togetherness
Family dysfunctional
Amazing deceitfulness
Among best of best
Strides on pride
Proud and fest
Plain indignity
Disaffection
Dissatisfaction
Distastefulness

Pretense togetherness
Family disgracefulness
Sad to see
So much family pain
Engulfed hypocrisy reign
Tarnished reputations
Personalities strained
Deleterious blame
Marked generations
To come
To follow

Ah ha!
Pretense togetherness
Family dysfunctional
Fight and fury
Fuss and disgust
Untrue stories and tales
Egoistic selfish duck
Everyone exasperating
Everyone venting
Misleading
Mistrusting
Misconstrued
Miscreant
Total misconduct
Total misconception

Pretense togetherness
Convenient forgetfulness
Utter ungratefulness
Pure unpleasantness
Insolent attitudes
Misguided fortitude
Family dysfunctional

Indubitable!
Pretense togetherness
Dearth contentment
Dearth discipline
No family principle
Lacks grace
Lacks love
No family principle
Requires truth

Family dysfunctional
Desires joy
Desires laughter
Desires love
No family principle
Needs faith
Hope
Charity
No family principle
Demands honesty

Yes Lord!
Pretense togetherness
Sadly dysfunctional
Your ear, Lord
May hear this wail
Your hand, Lord
May save this trail

Family dysfunctional
Household of many
Under the shelter
Pretense and honor
Family dysfunctional
Swim in shame
Family dysfunctional
Glorious frame
Lend your palm, Lord
To save the proud
In this dishonorable
Family dysfunctional

Pretense togetherness
Weighty load
Stomp and eradicate
That glaring pique
Lord, shower blessings
Of genuine embrace
Genuine friendship
Genuine happiness
Genuine smiles
On this
Family togetherness

At last!
Family togetherness
Discovers warm hearts
Family togetherness
Gives lasting joy
Family togetherness
Builds family unity
Family togetherness
Strengthens family ties

Divine Supreme Being
The Greater OM
The perfect example
We try to emulate
Infuse your serenity
And defuse
That circuit
And penetrate
That unwanted
Family dysfunctional
Peace!

Rosalind Severin McClean, November 1, 2014

SOME OF MY CONVENT SCHOOL MEMORIES IN ROSEAU, DOMINICA (DA),

THE SERIES

Preface

This series of five poems of some of my childhood memories at Convent School flashes a burst of light on the interest of the reader.

I wrote these poems with a slight twist of the Dominica (DA) dialect, using 'de' for 'the' and 'dey' for 'they,' to ensure that the reader is taken on a journey in real time.

Do enjoy this most pleasurable read.

Rosalind Severin McClean, August 29, 2020

Part I

"Teach your children early when they cannot say no."

MCMILLAN JNO-BAPTISTE (Dominica)

DE OLD ACADEMY

Montessori Class and First Division

Class of 1958
January was mine
Tots and dolls and pillow
School bag and recess
School uniform and beret
Perfect in size
Curious and sweet
Happiness

To school we go
In de Old Hillman
De best car rides
Slow in style
Convent School
Was de aim
And Virgin Lane
Made fame
In
De Old Academy

Ms. Garrad's class
Montessori it was
Sweet angel lady
We knew
Kindness and grace
All children face
Swept in her
Tender embrace

1 and 1 is 2
ABC in it too
Arts and crafts
Draw and color
Pencil and slate
Play and learn
Hands up in turn
We learnt it

Music and song
All band instruments
All children's chorus
All children singing
All children excited
Speech day to come
End of school year
We blossomed
We grew
In
De Old Academy

Ms. Bully's class
Gentle elegant lady
First Division
Was our mission
Some classmates
Yes permission
Roddy and Connie
Eric and Merina
Lincoln and Joanne
Among many

Oh! He forgot
0 plus 1 is 1
Lincoln on de blackboard
Stewart to de rescue
For de Arithmetic
Yes! It's true

Long thick black pencils
On paper we knew
To trace de Penmanship
And Arithmetic too
Dictation and Recitation
Spelling and Phonics
Rhythms and Rhymes
We learnt it

We sang many songs
And practiced happily
De little band instruments
De Clack Clack
Cymbals, Tambourines
Drums, Flutes, Triangles
Fat Wooden Sticks

Come Speech Day
With prizes
With acting and singing
When both classes
Sing with de little band

Come Speech day
To celebrate at
St. Gerard's Hall
Was de call

Come Speech Day
To mark de end
Of that sweet era
In
De Old Academy

Rosalind Severin McClean, July 11, 2014

OCEANS OF THOUGHTS

Part 2

"Train up a child in the way he should go: and when he is old, he will not depart from it."

PROVERBS 22:6

CONVENT SMALL SCHOOL

Second and Third Division

Anxious and anticipating
Second Division class awaiting
At de Convent
Wooden school building
De building so large
And exciting to see
Its long verandahs
And perfect views
Of de famous school yard
And hedges
And flowers too

New classrooms at best
With two in one
Brown wooden school desk
Where our schoolbooks
And pencils rest
More eagerness
More giggles
More focusing
More subjects
More studying

Our class so tight
Together alike
Ms. Stevenson so confident
And heading de class
One courageous afternoon
During an active lesson
Teacher called Rosalind
To the blackboard
To answer a question

Rosalind moved quick
And tripped over
Her brown schoolbag
From the bench
To the floor
She pitched

Oh no!
That burning bruise
Classmates alarmed
And teacher not amused
And rushed she did
To assist Rosalind
With that ghastly bruise
On her knee
Sweet compassion we knew
In
De Small School

Morning sunrise greeted
Another joyful year
Third Division class
With Ms. Laronde
As class teacher
And pleasant to meet

Her chattering pupils
Keen to learn
Composition and Dictation
English and Comprehension
Hygiene and Religion
Arithmetic too
More subjects
More homework
More test
That's correct!

School bell positioned
School recess in motion
School joys elevation
School timely fashioned
All pupils rushed out
From every corner
Every day
Yes! Recess bliss
Was de best time

It was divine
It was ball
It was play
All around
De big secured yard
In
De Small School

De Principal so tight
Her rule so might
Perfect and strict
Was her delight
Smiling Belgian nun in habit
Watch it!
Name auspicious
Sister Aloysius
Her movement continuous
From de school gate
To de classrooms
To her office
To school Mass

Oh yes!

Sister Aloysius

Element gem to greet

And sharp when meet

Sister's office in between

Third and Fourth Division

No omission

No mistake

No play

No way

'Twas lines

'Twas detention

'Twas punishment

'Twas cane

'Twas shame

In

De Small School

Rosalind Severin McClean, July 12, 2014

OCEANS OF THOUGHTS

Part 3

*"Foolishness is bound in the heart of a child; but the rod
of correction shall drive it far from him."*

PROVERBS 22:15

CONVENT SMALL SCHOOL

Fourth Division

Cheerful school buzz
Had begun
Small school children
Ran all over de grounds
Fourth Division pupils came
New school year?
Same head nun
New excitement?
Same school grounds
New friends?
Yes!
School buzz had begun
In
De Small School

New school uniform?
Same school drill
New classrooms?
Same school friends
New schoolbooks?
Same wooden desk

Yes!
School buzz
Had surely begun
In
De Small School

New class teacher
Stunning!
Skin of prune
Glowing beauty
It's gorgeous Ms. Peltier
To teach our Fourth Division class
So bright and sassy
So genuine and friendly
Qualities of sapphire
Sparkled!
An eventful year
In
De Small School

Her love and marriage
Fourth Division pupils knew
Her classroom buzzing
With wedding news
Roddy as page boy
To carry de ring
At Ms. Peltier's wedding

So sweet she was

To remember her children

Cubes of wedding cake

Basket full to celebrate

With her giggling

And happy pupils

Yes!

School buzz truly claimed

Mrs. Joseph her new name

Still!

We lovingly called her

Ms. Peltier

In

De Small School

Rosalind Severin McClean, November 19, 2018

OCEANS OF THOUGHTS

Part 4

"Apply thine heart unto instruction, and thine ears to the words of knowledge."

PROVERBS 23:12

CONVENT SMALL SCHOOL

Fifth Division

School holidays
Magnificent skies
Captivating summer but
Holidays seemed too short
Some of de school children
Returned at best
Two more blissful years
At Convent Small School
De old wooden building
Long and polished
Standing strong
With distinct character
In
De Small School

Convent school yard rowdy
Excitement was de mode
With teachers new and old
More courteous and enthused
Yes!
De classic head nun
Lovely Sister Aloysius
Welcoming all her pupils
Happily mixing
In her school yard

Expecting joyously
Fresh beginnings
Fresh classes
Fresh start
Fresh subjects
In
De Small School

It was Fifth Division
With Miss Alfred
Cheerfully preparing
In her spacious classroom
To teach her jolly pupils
Like Roddy and Merina
Like Charmaine and Joanne
Like Rosanne and Connie
Like Mary and Gillian
And others
Sitting side by side
Her pupils excited to learn
Those bigger academic
And challenging subjects

More quizzes

And more test

And even more strict

Yet we had plenty fun

In the midst

She taught us well

Throughout her role

Preparing us for

One more school year

In

De Small School

Rosalind Severin McClean, March 28, 2019

OCEANS OF THOUGHTS

Part 5

"The nature of the mind is such that it becomes what it thinks intensely upon."

SWAMI SIVANANDA

CONVENT SMALL SCHOOL

Six Division

Six Division class it was
With Miss Stevenson
Exemplary teacher
Slim and spunky
And cute as a bee
Standing in front de class
Her luck on point
To guide her pupils
To excel up
To Convent Big School

Academics to test
Arithmetic and English Literature
Geography and Science
And more compact subjects
To serious completion
Very focused she was
As her pupils faced
The last school year of
That Convent School era
In
De Small School

Beautiful lasting memories
Of childhood friendships
Beginning from
Miss Garrad's class
In de Old Academy
These gentle blessings
Of which we knew

Memories of school yards
Of childlike innocence
Of grace and purity
Of games and play
Of physical education
Of teams and plenty

Memories of classrooms
Of superb learning
Instilling lasting disciplines of old
Memories of the best teachers
Of intelligence and kindness
And honesty and trust

Memories of school assemblies
Each morning and afternoon
Sun hot, but we in de line
Some fainted, but we in de line
With giggles and smiles
And prayers and singing
And school announcements

Memories of our excellent
Speech Day celebrations
All pupils bright
Proud in their starched
Convent School uniforms
And some in
Pleated games uniforms

Memories of the end
Of each school year
With prize-giving
And school performances
And children singing
And children dancing

And with memories of myself
Playing classical music
To excellence
At our Speech Day ceremonies

And memories of myself
Accompanying Mrs. Cools-Lartigue
The devoted pianist to the school
And, enhancing my class chorus too
By playing piano duets
As they marched
From their seats
Up to the big stage
At the St. Gerard's Hall

And these were only some
Of my most beautiful memories
Of my Convent Small School era
In
De Small School

OM! Peace! OM!

Rosalind Severin McClean, March 28, 2019

DESCRIPTION OF THE OLD ACADEMY

The Old Academy, which was occupied by the Convent School, was located in Roseau across the street from the Catholic Bishop's residence on the corner of Virgin Lane, right at the top of Constitution Hill. The school was a dark grey-stone building with a high and long grey-stone wall that surrounded the property.

I remember clearly. There were two gates leading into the property of the school from Virgin Lane: a large wooden gate leading into the school yard, which we were not allowed to use; and a smaller iron gate leading to the front of the school building which was the main entrance to the school. There was also a verandah that stretched across the front of the school. There were large wooden brown windows which opened towards the verandah and towards the back of the school with black hooks to keep them open. A long wooden latch swung across the windows to lock them shut.

There were two classrooms: Ms. Garrard's class which was Montessori (kindergarten), and Ms. Bully's class which was First Division. There was a big doll which sat in full Convent School uniform on a small wooden chair in Ms. Bully's classroom. I attended both classes. In those days, the school year began in January. Pupils began school at three years old. I was not yet three years, but I was very alert and wanted to go to school. Yes, I went to school in full Convent School uniform, with my doll and my pillow and my recess (snack). The classes after Montessori were called Divisions. The school was run by the Catholic Belgian nuns.

There was a huge step at the back of the school which we, the pupils, were not allowed to use. This area was very cool; the location of the sun on the school building provided shade there, so during recess time some of the pupils would try to gather around that spot to play. That spot next to the step had no grass, but dusty small gravel. The teachers used to quickly call us away from that spot to the other side of the school because they couldn't see us there. I remember we sometimes practiced our little school band in the shade against the building facing the large school grounds. I also remember a big tree at the back of the school and benches under the tree.

The property's huge grassy lawn was pleasantly uneven, which was a hearty playground for all the pupils who attended the Old Academy.

Rosalind Severin McClean, September 10, 2020

OCEANS OF THOUGHTS

DESCRIPTION OF CONVENT SMALL SCHOOL

Convent Small School was situated in Roseau at the corner of Bath Road and Valley Road. The school was a long old brown wooden building with many doors and windows. There were also two verandahs, one on either side of the building facing the school yard and Valley Road, and the building was situated on the far side of the huge property towards Valley Road. The school was secured by a high stone wall which bordered Bath Road and Valley Road. There were sweet lime hedges and hibiscus hedges along the chicken wire fence that extended alongside the Botanical Gardens, and the other side of the school towards the Convent High School. The pupils were not allowed to pick the sweet limes and the flowers. We also had a little flower garden at the back of the building towards Valley Road.

The huge black Iron Gate to the main entrance of the school was on Bath Road. There were two smaller gates around the school. One was on Valley Road which the pupils and the teachers were forbidden to use. The other gate leading to the Botanical Gardens and the pathway leading to the Convent High School were used only when permission was given, although some pupils would occasionally run through and back on that pathway.

On entering the main school gate, pupils turned left to the big wooden step facing the Bath Road corner, which led to the back verandah of the front half of the school where the Second and Third Division pupils entered their classrooms. That half of the school was on a slightly higher level than the other half, with its verandah facing Valley Road. The principal's office sat in the middle of the building but on the higher level. A little ramp from the higher level connected the longer verandah of the second half of the school. Pupils took pleasure in running up and down the little ramp, hoping they would not get caught by the principal nun. Fourth, Fifth, and Sixth Division occupied the second level of the school. School assemblies were held in the yard and kept on the verandahs when it rained.

The school was broken down after the new Convent Prep was built, but the memories of Convent at the Old Academy and Convent Small School will live on in *Oceans of Thoughts*, Book One.

Rosalind Severin McClean, September 10, 2020

INSPIRATIONAL

Preface

One experiences the workings of Divine Intervention in their lives, according to their own capabilities and levels of understanding.

I was motivated to document one of my experiences through my work in poetry, captivating the stillness and guidance of Divine Intervention.

I was just not prepared for the directives that were coming through me at that time; however, the key at that moment was for me to know how to listen and to obey the guidance. The feeling at that moment was just unimaginable.

Sometimes we resist. Sometimes we do not comprehend the message.

Rosalind Severin McClean, August 31, 2020

"Kindness is honesty expressed with love.
A kind thought is better than a material gift because
it cannot be bought."

N. SRI RAM

GOD'S PEOPLE

Bustling public subway
Yet a bemused tedious
Lonely avenue
Two tall men
Years of forty
Fifty could be
Sons or brothers
Fathers or uncles
Someone's family
Veterans of wars
Service to country
What may be
Weak hands stretched out
Not a dime

Slouched against the walls
Unmoved they were
At the entrance of
Two crowded escalators
Of that busy
Transportation route
Phlegmatic
Impassive
Insouciant
Weak hands stretched out
Not a dime

Impetuous passengers
Hurried through
Line long like a mile
Undisturbed
Unperturbed
Unfazed
No one attentive
No one catechized
No one concerned
No one interested
Weak hands stretched out
Not a dime

Plain in sight
Those two men
Humble
Hungry
Look-alike
Despondent
Not a smile
Weak hands stretched out
Not a dime

One tall against the wall
One flopped over
On the subway platform
All heads down
Those two men
And all
My heart quivered
Seen one before, not two
I observed
Like in a vision
Strange emotions
My spirit shifted
Searched my tote I did
Up the escalator I drifted
My heart throbbed
"Think" I heard
HIS voice pounded
Then I remembered

Two brown paper bags
Individually wrapped
Unopened
Untouched
Were my breakfast and brunch
For work that Friday morning
Bought them in haste
Forgetting
Office breakfast and brunch
Purchased for the staff
For a celebrated day
Those sandwiches remained
To carry home
That Friday night

A smile broke in my heart
It was HIM who spoke
I rode that escalator
All the way up
Turned left at the landing
Took the down escalator
All the way back
To the subway platform
Where God's people stood
Weak hands stretched out
Not a dime

I approached God's people
Simultaneously
Retrieving from my sacoche
The two brown paper bags
Individually wrapped
Unopened
Untouched
I offered
Those two sandwiches
One each
To God's favored people
Weak hands stretched out
Not a dime

It was complete
Startled they were
Not a word
Fulfilling the mystery
Of the empyrean light
Saturated with nectar
In the Omniscient
Meditation of Consciousness
That Friday night, 7 p.m.

A mantra pulsated
I strode away
Towards the escalator
Back to the top landing
Contemplating
Man's unexplained karma
God's unexplained Grace
HIS voice vibrated
Like a thunder
"Don't look back"

My eyes pierced
Focused straight ahead
As the escalator climbed
To the upper platform
My being prayed
As I journeyed on
To my destination
Overwhelmed
With humility

A gratifying moment
Carefully orchestrated
With divine purpose
Of selfless service
An anointment
Neatly carved
With divine foresight
Of selfless giving
Epitomizing scripture
Realizing the promise
Of divine intention

God's people
Placed by appointment
Wrapped in the worldly frame
Of karma and obedience
Creating that profound space
Discerning that descriptive plan
To evolve that infirm mind set of
Weak hands stretched out
Not a dime

³Jah Bless! Peace!

Rosalind Severin McClean, October 12, 2013

---

³ JAH: God

Cracks in torrents of unintelligent lyrics from the youth to the senior spiral moments of strife that belch stench of disrespect

"I don't know you, so I don't have to respect you. Not because you are older than me I have to respect you."

Words that sit at the back of the tongue, taste of bad seed, saliva sip to the core, abash of prejudices and families.

Yet, carved to birth this message of inspiration.

Those written stains cannot be erased.

May the Lord of Creation dissolve the burden of unfavored disrespect.

Rosalind Severin McClean, August 29, 2020

Preface

I wrote this poem in meditation as a tool to enlighten one's heart around our seniors.

The loss of respect hanging over the mouths of generations for seniors must be noted, and through some upliftment of the Word one might reflect on the self.

This poem is written with an emphasis on one of my favorite books of the Bible, the Epistle of James.

As I look towards Jehovah Shalom, 'the Lord of Peace,' I gather the inspiration, the strength and wisdom to write this song.

Rosalind Severin McClean, August 27, 2020

"James, a bondservant of God and of the Lord Jesus Christ, to the twelve tribes which are scattered abroad: Greetings. My brethren, count it all joy when you fall into various trials."

JAMES 1:1-2

I AM SENIOR

I am senior
I am family
I am senior
I am a relative
I am senior
I am a gift
I am senior

"Every good gift and
Every perfect gift
Is from above
And comes down from
The Father of lights
With whom there is
No variation or shadow
Of turning"
(James 1:17)

I am senior
I am family
I am senior
I am a relative
I am senior
I am an inspiration
I am senior

"If anyone among you
Thinks he is religious
And does not bridle his tongue
But deceives his own heart
This one's religion is useless"
(James 1:26)

I am senior
I am family
I am senior
I am a relative
I am senior
I am inspired
I am senior

"And the tongue is a fire
A world of iniquity
The tongue is so set
Among our members
That it defiles the whole body
And sets on fire
The course of nature
And it is set on fire by hell"
(James 3:6)

I am senior
I am family
I am senior
I am a relative
I am senior
I am an observer
I am senior

"But no man can tame the tongue
It is an unruly evil
Full of deadly poison
With it we bless
Our God and Father
And with it we curse men
Who have been made
In the similitude of God"
(James 3:8-9)

I am senior
I am family
I am senior
I am a relative
I am senior
I am respected
I am senior

"Out of the same mouth
Proceed blessings and cursing
My brethren
These things ought
Not to be so"
(James 3:10)

I am senior

I am family

I am senior

I am a relative

I am senior

I am wise

I am senior

"Can a fig tree, my brethren

Bear olives, or

A grapevine bear figs?

Thus, no spring yields

Both salt water and fresh"

(James 3:12)

I am senior

I am family

I am senior

I am a relative

I am senior

I am wisdom

I am senior

"But the wisdom
That is from above
Is first pure
Then peaceable, gentle
Willing to yield
Full of mercy and good fruits
Without partiality and
Without hypocrisy"
(James 3:17)

I am senior
I am family
I am senior
I am a relative
I am senior
I am That
I am senior
I AM THAT

Peace! The Greatest OM!

Rosalind Severin McClean, August 27, 2020

My sister, Mrs. Yvonne Volney

Yvonne wearing a stunning head piece made from
madras at the Dominica Creole Festival

When Yvonne wore her daughter Sharlene's national
dress during the Creole Festival of Dominica

View of the southern tip of Dominica

Scotts Head, Dominica

Rosalind Severin McClean

A view of Roseau, the capital of Dominica with Mount
Trois Piton towering over

The Old Academy building today, 2020. Pictures of the original Old Academy building were lost due to various hurricanes over the years

Montessori children sitting on the back verandah of
Convent Small School in 1957

School children sitting on the front verandah of
Convent Small School in the 1960s

Made by Major Richards Mission of Mercy

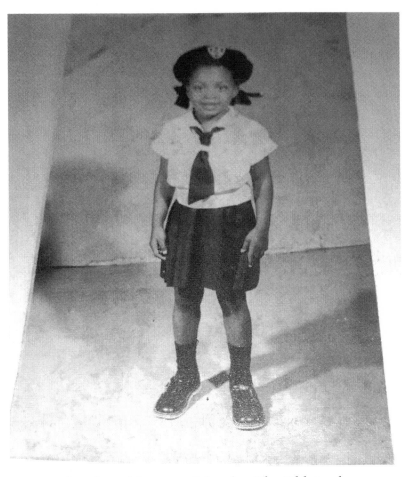

My first day of Convent School at The Old Academy,
in full Convent uniform in 1958

My mother, my sister Carol and I attending a
children's costume party

ABOUT THE AUTHOR

Rosalind Severin McClean has been known for her profound and most inspiring writing style. Her impressive work in poetry has claimed excellent reviews from her many audiences, both local and international. Not only has she participated in open-mic events and written editions in newspaper articles to showcase her work, but she is also an exemplary performer in the arts, dance and culture. Her natural gift as an author was recognized from childhood, but now as a senior she has decided to publish Book One of her *Oceans of Thoughts* series.

Born in the Commonwealth of Dominica, Ms. McClean lives with her daughter Malti in Queens, New York.

Made in the USA
Middletown, DE
24 February 2022

61710437R00097